Helen Moore is an award-winning B
currently based in Sydney. Her debu
Living Margins (Shearsman Books, 2(
tradition of visionary politics in Bri
manent Publications, 2015), which r
thropocene' epoch, has been acclain
as 'a milestone in the journey of ecop
English work, *INTATTO. INTACT*, was published by La Vita Felice in 2017.
Helen regularly reads her work at literary and environmental events, and
facilitates ecopoetry workshops and seminars. As a socially engaged artist,
she leads creative writing programmes to support health and well-being in
the community and has collaborated on a range of ecologically oriented
community projects with artists from various disciplines.

'I love the vastness of Helen Moore's vision and the unflinching way she puts
it into the world, her tone urgent, language impassioned. *The Mother Country*
spells out the cost of our man-made, consumer culture to all who have been
dispossessed and displaced – indigenous peoples, women, the earth, its crea-
tures. 'The Disinherited' is a particularly brilliant and fearless section, indict-
ing colonial politics in Australia and Scotland. But Moore's Blakean vision,
tackling the toxic tyrannies of our own times, is always tempered by minute
details which convey her deep love for what is under threat: lichen "pale as
snuff"; swifts that "sleep on the wing"; the generations who will inherit our
broken world – "What crumbs will we leave them?"' *Rosie Jackson*

'Helen Moore harnesses flexible patterns of verse to assimilate and contain
her own painful experience of being disinherited by using it to intensify her
already strong empathic powers in a way that resonates with the grief, histor-
ical and present, of the wider world. The acuity of her critical intellect, the
accuracy of her sensory observations, and her skill at wielding, and retrieving,
the resources of language lift the poems above the level of a generalized la-
ment. She makes us see, hear and experience not only the grief of things
across the planet but also the memories of the damaged and vanished worlds
from which it rises. Perhaps in these perilous transitional times we are all
disinherited now, and Moore's poems perform an important duty by making
us feel the pathos and the righteous rage of that condition.' *Lindsay Clarke*

'In these verbally dextrous, deeply rooted poems, Helen Moore demonstrates
the truth of her quotation from Blake: "*A tear is an intellectual thing.*" She
knows that truth can only be approached by emotion as well as by think-
ing. (She has a fine line in satire.) She is not only knowledgeable – about Aus-
tralia's colonising, the Scottish clearances, the world's ecologies – she is also
very courageous, confronting with wit and imagination, anger and profound
grief the reality of the crisis our wonderful planet and all of us on it are ap-
proaching. (Her personal painful experience of being "disinherited" by a
mother she loved and pitied gives her additional keys to the many emotions
involved.) If our world is to awaken to its own danger, it will need ecopoets
such as Moore.' *D.M. Black*

THE MOTHER COUNTRY

Helen Moore

AWEN

Stroud

First published in 2019 by Awen Publications
12 Belle Vue Close, Stroud GL5 1ND, England
www.awenpublications.co.uk

Front cover image: *Captive*, a sculpture by Marian Bruce
www.marianbruce.co.uk
Photo: David Oakley

Cover design: Kirsty Hartsiotis
Editing: Anthony Nanson

ISBN 978-1-906900-58-8

For more information about Helen Moore visit:
www.helenmoorepoet.com

For all the disinherited,
human & other-than-human

'I have deliberately excluded my daughter, Helen Louise Moore, from this my Will and it is my intention that the said Helen Louise Moore should receive no part of my estate.'

The Last Will & Testament of Elizabeth Jane Moore,
27 August 2013

CONTENTS

IV. LEGACIES

I. THE DISINHERITED

'In the colonies the truth stood naked, but the citizens of the mother country preferred it with clothes on; the native had to love them, something in the way mothers are loved.'

Frantz Fanon, *The Wretched of the Earth*

'From what I have said of the Natives ... they may appear to some to be the most wretched people upon earth, but in reality they are far more happier than we Europeans.'

James Cook, *The Journals of Captain James Cook on His Voyages of Discovery*

BIOPHONY, PRIOR TO INVASION

Waran, 1787

Here, at the edge of day, the land articulates a wild music to
assure itself that it has stayed, despite night's perpetual wash, the
thieving of shadows.

Resuming its rounds, Sun glitters the Pacific rim as Kookaburrah,
Currawong, Whipbird, Crow, Magpie Goose, Galah, Lorikeet,
Cockatoo, Emu, Brolga, Frog, Cicada sing it up. A unique colour
springing from the throat of each – at dawn's advance, variant
hues & tones infuse the land.

Song gilding the creams & yellows of sandstone. Song greening
coverts, silvering branches, trunks. Song lightening the Crab-
holed mud of Mangrove, Saltmarsh. Song above all defining the
soul of the cove.

No one voice displaces another, whilst the orchestration –
improvised through evolutionary time – resonates with call &
response. Amongst it all, people sit by the smoking embers of
their fires. Drawing breath into their lungs, they pour sonic
rainbows into country, communing with ancestral lines unbroken
for 20,000 generations.

THE MOTHER COUNTRY

England, 1787

What sort of 'mother'
        cuts off her offspring,
casts them away
        in ships to a land
she claims
        belongs to no one?
('Terra nullius',
        out there – beyond the Indian Ocean –
'New South Wales'
        has a few *'natives'*, is barely on the map.)

Heart of cut glass,
        a mother craving
her next fix
        (gold, coal, wool, flax,
timber); & with her
        hulks & prisons filled, her
American colonies
        raising fists – into a new fleet she packs
prisoners in leg irons
        locked down in the hold.

From the Mother-
        bank, she waves them away
(the invisible hand's
        two-finger salute) as she's conveyed to London,
grinding the poor
        beneath the wheels of her carriage,
kicking with her silk
        brocade slippers those *'gutter-snipes'* obliged

to pilfer, to sell

        their bodies to survive.

              At 'the great square of Venus',

Britannia enters

        the bawdy house she keeps for lords, princes,

sucks them

        for their worth, flogs them with her whip,

& takes a pipe

        of opium to unwind.

              Later, in a giant wig sporting

rigged miniatures

        of her ships, she cavorts at a palace

masquerade; &

        in the bedchamber of 'the old, mad king'

ensures he'll do her

        every bidding …

'FIRST CONTACT'

Botany Bay, 1788

Evokes
          delicacy
                    Self extending
to explore
               Other
                        skin-enfolded
nerves
          feeling a flower's
                    plush curve
nostrils flared
          to hoard
               its wily perfume.
Or that moment when
               a moony throb of milk & wind
                          opens
             to mama's vivid eyes
emits
      a cry of pleasure
               ('*We are all Stone Age children*' – R.D. Laing).

Imagine, instead, Michelangelo's
               hoary-headed God
         in white robes,
His finger
         condescending
             to Adam –
                  in this frame
depicted as
         black –
naked, *Manly*
         (his body

no
Renaissance fetish ...
just untouched
by 'Civilisation').
This Adam whose response
to bewigged naval officers
(polished buttons
tricorne hats, loaded muskets)
stepping from the surf
like camp, sexless
ghosts
is perhaps
cautious curiosity?

A BRITISH MARINE OFFICER CONSIDERS THE COLONIAL PRESENCE, VENTRILOQUISING THE 'NATIVES'

> 'a people for whom I cannot but feel some share of affection'
>
> Lieutenant-General Watkin Tench

Port Jackson, 1788

Ghostly quiet their crew arrived, a flock of huge boats
with three stripped trees standing aloft. Hung from these
were misty webs, which gather up the wind

to draw these 'ships' across the sea. With what seemed
charred lumps upon their heads (that they name 'hat'),
their warriors drove a tall spike into the earth. From it fly colours

of their place – red, white, blue. Putting captives to work
is what they do. From the boats' vast bellies poured a sickly crowd
in heavy, clanking ropes, skin & hair riddled with insects.

Some of these unfortunates could only crawl on to the shore,
while others lay & groaned like speared fish.
The night they got here, the portent of a storm –

thunderbolts & lightning stabbing at the sky. From the cove
shrieks & wails were heard, as if they were dying; then
came howling as they danced, & sounds of mating until dawn.

In their mouths many bear a bulbous thing with fire;
it sends smoke streaming from their nostrils & appears
to slow them down, makes them smile a little more.

As does their drink – throat-burning liquid called 'To the King!'
They're keen to press us with it, but we spit this poison out.
Gulping cupfuls, they roar, feign fearlessness, & soon tumble down.

At first, we didn't know female from male – most lack beards
& keep their bodies hidden. But those who don't cover both
their legs together pull a pale penis out to piss.

We've seen males rub a sharp tool on cheeks & chin
to remove the facial hair; a few are skilled at this –
such cutters are called 'barber', & the bravest of our lot

bring necks & faces to their 'razor'. Their pallid women
frequent the shade, sigh at moving doubles of themselves
in hard, flashing pools called 'looking glass'. Why is unclear –

though it fans the embers in their men, whom they watch erecting
small sorts of shelters. Struggling in the heat, it seems
the men have urgent needs to copulate, as if half-starved of it.

Their warriors bear fire-sticks that can fell birds from the sky
(& which they point at us if we take their things for ourselves).
Mounted upon high-hoofed creatures with long, hairy tails,

they stroll about & flick reedy serpents on to the captives. Jumping
& cracking, these stop them heeding their sexual hunger.
Such is this new, white 'society' …

'A TEAR IS AN INTELLECTUAL THING'

William Blake's engraving *A Family of New South Wales* was commissioned for John Hunter's *Historical Journal of the Transactions at Port Jackson and Norfolk Island* and based on a sketch by Governor Philip Gidley King.

Lambeth, 1792

Down at Hercules Buildings, Blake works his creaking press,
both hands heaving the spokes – like Vitruvian Man's
the wheel's wooden limbs outstretched.

Warmed by his exertion, the artist sheds coat and bonnet rouge;
then, from the press's bed, lifts the woollen blanket, peels
the inked paper from the copper plate, and moves

for light beside a casement opened on to the Garden of Love.
(There with Catherine, his wife, he delights in being
as God made them amongst Herbs, Roses, Doves,

and, falling on their skin, Albion's sunrays, rain.) Now seeing
his engraving beside King's original, Blake grins, gratified
with his rendition. *'When I from black and he from white cloud free ...'*

Passing through the landscape with dignity, this vision
of a *'noble'* family, indeed – unclothed and carrying tools
of their existence (fishing kit, spears, shield), the son

the spit of his father, and on her mother's shoulders
their small daughter. It's just four years since the British
landed, yet, unbeknownst to Blake, the family survives solely

on paper. As mordant that bites into the plate, makes hollows,
pocks, sunken lines, craters, European disease has ravaged
local people – their unburied dead like driftwood strewn in coves.

On the table that's anvil to Blake's imagination and craft,
he considers another finished commission. Two dark-skinned girls
flank one white – her winding rope at second glance

binding the pair: 'Europe supported by Africa and America', a
    standing
to which the latest colony will advance. Struck by intimations
of the truth this means, the artist weeps. *'A tear is an intellectual thing.'*

DAUGHTER OF THE DISSOLUTION

Sydney, 2016

1. 'Derelict'

      Corner of Pitt & Market Streets, &
of European descent, he's anchored on a crate,
      a 'tinny' plus a torn *Sydney*

Morning Herald in his tattooed hands,
      a piebald companion moored to his ankle –
a Jackahuahua, by the look of it.

      Amidst currents of shoppers trailing
designer bags, & slick
      workers escaping for a latte & a smoke,

this fixed point in the Central Business District,
      this mute greybeard, cap backwards on a greasy head,
legs with an unwashed patchwork effect.

      At the exact spot where a stream
had its source, sparkled covewards,
      it seems the dispossessed take root –

daughter of the dissolution, *'Cora Gooseberry'*
      (as colonists dubbed her),
in middle age sat here on the footpath,

      a clay pipe in her mouth,
with headscarf, magistrate-issue blanket, & wearing
      a colonial breastplate inscribed, *'Queen of Sydney'*.

Like the introduced fruit,
        synonymous with being prickly, out
of place, 'Cora' was a 'character', butt

        of bigot jokes, artists' pet subject.
Sketched with the corners of her mouth pulled down,
        the lines a dowsing rod

pointing to the firewater anaesthetising
        her veins. Rum, which kept the colony
afloat, slugged from a copper mug,

        a State-owned curio in which her daily 'allowance'
was obtained. A cesspit within four years
        of the British flag, the stream is not quite forgotten –

through its dismal culvert, it trickles
        down to the harbour,
is a buried thread of history.

2. Kaaroo

Born in the year prior to invasion, originally Kaaroo
        may have been wrapped in paperbark,
its native creaminess peeled in sheets from the tree.

        Cherished at her wiyanga's breast,
with milk infusing her veins,
        & carried everywhere,

Kaaroo would have first discovered life
        skin to skin with others.
From the snuggle of her mother's shoulders,

dream-snakes of moonlight
on water, tendrils of smoke, & embers
            winking in the base of the canoe …

slow rocking up through mama's body,
            & the keen aromas of charring Bream.
Often the wiry beard of her biyanga

            (a tribal chief called Moorooboora)
tickling her cheeks;
            & the strong, pliant hands of women –

aunties, cousins dillying with her,
            rubbing her limbs, her plump belly
burnished like damun.

            Oiled to withstand the Sun's brand,
Kaaroo grew bold & curious
            began to crawl, stand –

a small being who'd love & bleed,
            taste the earth's flavours,
her first words arising from them.

3. Mother Tongue

'The woods, exclusive of the animals which they
occasionally find in their neighbourhood, afford
them but little sustenance.'
            Captain David Collins, Deputy Judge Advocate of
                                    New South Wales, 1798

Of the Dharug language,   only a few hundred words remain …

            Yurungi   wild duck

Mirral   crested pigeon

Bunmarra   lizard

Midiny   yam

Damun   Port Jackson fig

Danganuwa   tasty worm

Warrigal   greens

Guragura   possum

Gurgi   bracken root

Midjurburi   lilly-pilly (fruit)

Wadanggari   heather banksia (nectar)

Gaban   egg

Gadyibelang

good to eat

WHITEFELLA FISHING

Mrs Macquarie's Point, Sydney, 2016

Just a little east of Sydney Harbour Bridge
(a huge coat-hanger minus its hook, which fizzed up
seven million dollars on New Year's Eve),
a man's straddling his 'esky', down beside a rock pool –

tanned limbs, feet, white collar open, shirt sleeves
rolled, hat a low cross-hatch pattern, his knife flicking
sequins off a limp fish, while Gulls hover like drones
the rich kids got for Christmas.

Laying out the Flathead before him, he snaps it on his smartphone
(*'a good'un'* for uploading to *Anglers' Forum*)
as a bunch of Chinese tourists, hunting 'The Spectacle',
swarms for selfies with a 'quintessential local' –

the laconic Aussie, whose forbears bashed the bush, pushing
ever west (forest supplanted by millions of 'four-legged clansmen'),
the legacy this leisure
our man now takes for granted.

Overhead, a rumbling seaplane with twin sleds,
while, up the Parramatta, Captain Cook Cruises
travels eastwards to sea with a white, washing wake –
a wake to erase the shadows rippling in these waves.

*

Back seven generations, for countless time
back in the day, when Flathead was 'Marrinagul',
when flowering Bloodwood, calling Cicadas
meant Oysters were plump, Bream on the bite …

15

as off these rocks Cadigal women
observant, singing,
cast handwoven lines from slender canoes,
shell-hooks baited with cockles.

*

'WATCH   TOUR   EAT   DRINK   SHOP'

instructs an Opera House marketing concept
as late afternoon bakes the white architectural sails.

His catch cool inside the blue plastic box,
our fisher returns to his bijou urban garden, fires up the barbie,
opens a chilled Sauvignon Blanc.

Picking his back teeth, he'll see the Sun set with nonchalance
to threads pervading his phone, anglers' talk
of government warnings, 'high levels of dioxins'.

And still he'll think how smart he's been
to catch his dinner just a little east
of Sydney Harbour Bridge.

TRAFFICKED WOMEN DROWN OFF FRENCH COAST

A reconstruction, 1833

A ship with 108 women, 12 children, & 16 crew on board has sunk at Boulogne-sur-Mer, a French port close to Calais. Three members of crew were the sole survivors. Under the command of Captain John Hunter, the *Amphitrite*, a 200-ton ship bound for New South Wales, set sail from Woolwich on 25 August, with ship's surgeon, Dr Forrester, overseeing the live cargo. Six days later in severe gales the *Amphitrite* ran aground at low tide on Boulogne's harbour sands.

Local sailors offered rescue, but Captain Hunter rejected all assistance, stating he could only land in Botany Bay. One survivor, boatswain John Owen, told how the women packed below smashed through the half deck-hatch, begging captain & surgeon to launch the longboat. At flood tide on the evening of 31 August, waves broke the *Amphitrite* in two. Hunter & Forrester drowned along with all but three crew who climbed the spars & clung to wreckage.

Members of the French Marine Humane Society recovered the dead. An eyewitness said, *'I never saw so many fine & beautiful bodies … Some of the women were the most perfectly made; & French & English wept together at such horrible loss of life …'*

With crime rates soaring in Britain's industrialising cities, thousands of people have been found guilty of petty crimes & flung to far corners of the Empire. Some *Amphitrite* women were economic migrants, seeking better lives elsewhere. Maria Hoskins, 28, jailed at Newgate for stealing a watch, was revealed to have told PC Broderick that she was denied aid from Covent Garden's poor relief, & that, *'if … not transported for … theft, she would commit something more heinous that would send her out of the country'.*

Boatswain Owen described opening a trunk at Boulogne's Bureau de la Marine. Its sodden contents included *'small arrangements for future employment & housewifery, the little flat iron, the neat store of needles, pins, cotton, etc.'*, which most women brought with them.

A third of *Amphitrite*'s victims were from Scotland, where *'ridding the land of Scotch-Celts'* has displaced numerous Highlanders into the cities. Many refugees speak no English & struggle to find work & housing. Reports suggest entire families are camping out on Glasgow Green near the public gallows. The homeless run the risk of being charged with vagrancy, for which the penalty can be transportation.

BLACK HOUSE, GREAT BERNERAY, WESTERN ISLES

''s na h-igheanan nam 'badan sàmhach / a' dol a
Clachan mar o thus'

July 2016

Squat dwelling of the old ways, stone buttock bared to the grey
Sound of Harris; roof timbers exposed; thatch a scalp with
alopecia. From the roof-tree (sea-salvaged beams, white and
crooked as the shins of old men), handmade ropes sway – doll's
hair ragged by Atlantic winds.

Dreich hole for shelter. Mud floor tramped by Sheep, who stamp
in at a door jilted on hinges. Here, the walls' depth measures
roughly a woman's length when knocked down, arms out,
resisting eviction.

Modernity's groomed the place in other ways too. But the panel-
clad interior has been reduced to a jumble of tongue & groove
littering rooms – its greens, pinks, and creams bruised by the
elements. Tangle of rot and weather.

A stove made the warm bosom of this house; now it's a rusting
hulk slumped by which the sole settee is a broken defiance of
springs, stuffing of horsehair plucked out for nests. One culprit
Wren flees through a window's jagged teeth, where Nettles jostle
like aggrieved kin barred from re-entering.

Proud, bristling emblem of Scotland, Thistles guard these ruins
and, a stone's throw back across the cropped machair, other
homes that formed the clachan. Two have been restored for
tourists exploring the island, their walls fresh white. Like the
lead-hemmed gowns of Victoria and her entourage (cruising by
the famined isles in 1847), their thatch is weighted against gales.

Secured with blue polyprop round the coarse roof of each,
perhaps three dozen flat pendulous stones. And do the visitors
see them, these petrified livers and kidneys? Hung out to dry
here, so many dull livers and lungs, and countless grey, grey
hearts of the emigrants – the vital Gaelic cut away.

TEENAGE SKATE PUNK

'For tens of thousands of years tribal people every-
where have greeted the onset of puberty, especially
in males, with elaborate and excruciating initiations –
a practice that plainly wouldn't have been necessary
unless their young were as extreme as ours.'
Michael Ventura, *The Age of Endarkenment*

An 80s suburban kid of MacDonald heritage, in cap, pants, singlet,
off his face with his mates freestyling
on acid – a waft of Frangipani, its high, heady scent
pervading molten Christmas streets.

Gyrating past a Pelican with a pink Pinocchio nose for its beak,
Alba's body like water, as tarmac rolling up in waves,
as tinsel twinkling from Fig trees,
as fake snow round windows,
as Rudolph on fly-screens,
& Santa bleeding out on Mrs Wong's veranda.

A muscled charisma affecting *'no worries'*, Alba flew
atop this board that shook him loose of most taboos.
Then with The Oils, The Hard-Ons, Kiss, Sex Pistols
(rebel men he put upon a pedestal)
adrenalin & speed gained a soundtrack as he gave
the finger to priests, cops, teachers –
the shapes they tried to cookie-cut him into.

His folks bought his first car, a Holden Torana …
within weeks, a drunken chase in the old government Domain …
giving gas, blasting out to where Macquarie's wife
watched for English ships (& gloated
at the thought of prisoners on Pinchgut) …

until a rocky outcrop brought him up short –
                    twisted metal & a vicious rash of glass
how Alba faced the music.

Describing this misadventure, in middle age he still
            drags a chain – the guilt he owns as work-in-progress,
& the legacy of a culture
                        lacking guided rites of passage.

Uncanny, though, this crash site that unconsciously he chose …
            close to Sydney's Opera House, near Woccanmagully –
                    where foreign seed first colonised the land
                            as 'First Farm' – but which was

        always sacred bora ground for karadjis
                    initiating young men
                            as warriors & hunters.

'A STATE OF POSSESSION ALREADY EXISTING BEYOND THE MEMORY OF [HU]MAN[S]'

'It will manifestly be rendering essential service to
the tenantry and lower classes of cottagers in this
district to deprive them of the privilege of
misspending ... so much of their time and labour ...
in collecting their miserable turf for firing, which is
the chief and in fact the only benefit ... that they reap
from this common.'

Sir John Sinclair, re the Commonty of Millbuie,
Scotland, 1795

The commonty for building the complete
house: stones, clay for mortar, timber roofing & fixtures,
the fail & divot for walls/roofs, & a fine selection
of renewable thatches: heather, broom, rushes, bracken.

The commonty for fuel: peat & turf, gorse & broom,
sometimes wood, occasionally coal. At the heart
of the house, the hearth rarely extinguished, extending
warmth & heat for drying, boiling, cooking.

The commonty for grazings, & from Beltane the flitting
of women & children to the sweet meadow grasses
up at the shieling. Lumbering tongues of black Cattle
browsing flowers; rich milk in butter, cheeses, songs.

The commonty for mulching the kailyard: kelp, limestone,
marl, & turf. For cordage, the commonty's Heather & Reeds;
the Birch, Rowan, Ash from the commonty for carving
quaichs, spoons, spindles, pipes, spurtles.

The commonty for yielding food & natural medicine:
sap, blossoms, leaves, berries, roots, mushrooms;

tonics of Heather & Thyme; Nettles rubbed on rheumatic
knees or cooked up for broth; root of Tormentil for fever.

The commonty for water: drinking, washing, work
at the clear-sighted burn; for dye plants, the commonty's
colour-map in the warp & weft of the plaid. For
comings & goings the commonty; markets, fairs, worship.

BLOCK HEADS

'Phrenology was not just an example of Victorian
arrogance, it epitomised the way in which the
language of colonization obscured its real impulses.'
Don Watson, *Caledonia Australis*

Crumpled from luggage that's flown Scotland–
Australia, I soak a cross-hatch of dun fibres
in a bowl of water, reshape my hat
on a milliner's block.

Relict in the in-laws' home for over half
a century – full dome, this heavy cranium's worn
crown is cracked, pitted, its dark tan
(jelutong logged from Malaysia, Borneo, Sumatra)
gouged by tacks & pins stuck in to fix some point
d'esprit lace to white
oriental satin, embroidered net
to satin charmeuse.

The milliner's name is scorched into the base:
'E.F. Chegwidden'. Online, a black & white image
of a youthful Caucasian head
modelling a hat   (cloche style, Twenties).

And was it E.F.'s ad in Sydney's *Sunday Times*, 1911:
        'Beautiful racing hats of Tagal,
        trimmed smartly with flowers …
        two guineas'?

Two guineas?
Perhaps the skull of *'a young Australian female'*
sent home by Sir Thomas Mitchell, a Scotsman,
fetched more   *'for the uncannily fine set of teeth'*?

Such demand flourished beyond the Victorians,
and body parts of First Australians still languish
in archives of British museums.

Others have been repatriated,
but awaiting reparations   remain

            'grave responsibilities' for curators.

NIGHT TRAIN, MELBOURNE TO SYDNEY

At the centre of our universe, our hands,
fine adjustment of fingers & thumbs to find
just the degree of comfort – a crumb afforded us
at this raked angle, economy class,
backs aching, buttocks numbed, the rattling
inter-carriage door & staggering snores
of the walrus-man in front, as we pound along
inside the belly of this beast, XPT racing
through vast open spaces, its steel flanks illumined
subtly by the Moon, which waxes in reverse here
on the far side of the world. Out there, Stars,
Roos, Snakes ... the dizzying ache
of half-conquered wilderness & a glowing alarm –
level-crossing lights flash at Benalla:
Ding-ding, ding-ding, ding-ding! (No car waiting.)
At Albury we cross the Victorian border, the state
name enshrining the Mother Country's power ...
(How is it to have to reference this in today's Australia?)
Wagga Wagga, Tumlong, Junee – from Cootamundra
night's rife with sensationalised danger
(*I'm a Celebrity ... Get Me out of Here!*) – this land
where, eight generations since invasion, Kooris
still feel the pain, fight for justice, title, & sovereignty.
Boarding the train at Southern Cross station, we saw
banners proclaiming, 'WE DO NOT BELONG
HERE!' & marvelled at the irony of this ad
for the new *King Kong* movie.
But my mind's eye still projects Brook Andrew's show
at Federation Square. In *The Right to Offend
Is Sacred*, his archived cartoons
unpack a history of caricaturing racism;
& in the gallery space adjacent, his avenue

of *Gun-Metal Grey* ethnographic portraits
with dark heads glimmering as if on a night such as this.
At one end I watched monitors with film
of a white woman's operatic singing, while opposite this
an outsize gramophone horn, beyond which –
as if collapsed while trying to speak –
a skeleton lay in pieces inside a glass cabinet, textbook
Craniology of Aborigines on the shelf below.
The night train winds through the vast plains
of pastoralists, who brought their 'Big Merinos' & left
country parched, dusty … creek-beds worn-out bullock whips.
Sometimes rails parallel highway as we outstrip
sinuous road trains – fiendish eyes dwindling into darkness.
Then, up alongside, looming hulks of freight-cars,
sides grotesque laceworks of graffiti.
At Goulburn – known for its 'Supermax'
Prison – Rocky Hill Memorial wheels an eerie beacon
for the Australian War Dead, killed fighting battles for Europe,
its giant beam slicing up the night.
But what memorials for Indigenous people
who died defending themselves & country
on countless internal frontiers?
(How many lives?)
As dawn spreads its pyre across the sky,
Moss Vale, Campbelltown, & on up
to Sydney's sprawling suburbs
from where the morning commute is already underway.
Here, like uncontrolled fire,
high-wired rents force the dispossessed
far beyond the margins …
Woolworths warehouses, late-night 'bottlos', remnant bush.

II. THE GATES OF GRIEF

'To speak of sorrow
works upon it
            moves it from its
crouched place barring
the way to and from the soul's hall.'
                    Denise Levertov, 'The Sorrow Dance'

THE CHANGELING

Between the taut, beige suspension bridge
& junctions of her bra, my mother's flesh
was pressed into plump hills & sparsely
wooded valleys, her skin pale & freckled
like an inverse Milky Way.

Once in a while I'd climb on to her dressing
table stool, alone with her reflected
in the triptych of mirror, watching
as she'd strip to high-waisted knickers

to scrub her pits in the corner sink,
while I pretended to play
with the large roller brush
she used to restructure her perm.
(Or I'd be allowed a dab of Oil of Ulay
to pat into my cheeks.) Those moments
were the greatest intimacy I recall.

Mostly there was her being 'kissy-kissy'
with my little brother ... the reef
of her nose, his small, nostrilled sucker,
their lip-to-lip underwater meeting ...

& I inside a diving suit & mask
numbly observing. That solemn girl
who never felt *quite* her mother's flesh & blood.

ALONE WITH THE CORPSE

After my father's death,
we're motionless
inside the frame of mythic time –
mother & grown-up daughter
alone with the corpse,
a cameo of lace,
the chill clay of the face
(made up as if he's sleeping),
& his silver thatch
misstyled by morticians.
I speak of this &, to recognise him
better, my hands remake the parting,
Mother breathing alongside,
her faltering words:
He was a good man …
Naming his qualities, I agree,
though needing balance, add,
But he was hard on you too –
he must have hurt you many times,
as I take her in my arms,
&, barely believing this moment
to be real, say that I love her.
I should have left it at that;
but, hoping for the healing
that can come through
bereavement, I repeat
a few words of this
a while later.
Imperious as
a queen towards
a heresy, she retorts
(a portcullis crashing

down between us,
& I held captive),
We don't speak ill
of the dead!

HELIUM GIRL

Nights he was late, she became a giant ear,
every fibre, every cell straining like a trumpet

ravenous for sounds, a flower that imbibed,
digested any hint of his return …

the distant swish of traffic, that engine-thrum
singling out the road, its tortoise-style

approach, the ecstatic crunch of gravel, tyres
rolling towards rest, while headlights

glancing through the curtained room
seemed a pair of herald angels to announce

his delivery from darkness. Then finally
this little girl, pent up in bed with Pink Teddy

clutched to her chest, could close her mollusc
eyes, sigh as if attaining benediction,

and with no goodnight kiss, no whispered
I-love-yous, fall into the bliss of non-separation.

                              *

Sometimes as she lay waiting, she'd leave her body –
a loosed balloon drifting in the dull expanse,
nudging the ceiling, bouncing up against it

as helium girl come top of her box.
Or she'd flit like Daddy-long-legs, those
martyred clowns, whose relics

her little brother would excise to place
upon her pillow. Hanging out with these maimed
creatures, she'd stare at the small figure

lying on the narrow shelf of bed –
a fly-on-the wall view of some other body
on a ward trolley – and darkly slip back in.

*

At last when sleep came, there'd be this dream –
her riding in the back of daddy's car, the sleek machine

zooming into night, dashboard lights, electric windows,
mummy's snores, daddy pressing cruise control,

and slowly rising, lifting from the seat,
her body sucked through the rear windscreen,

left a hovering ghost above the motorway,
voice on mute, outstretched arms in futile ache

towards the number plate, those red demonic eyes
vanished into night, all oblivious to her plight,

and daddy forever driving out of her existence …

THE BIG C

1. Three Oncologists

After the painting by Ken Currie, Scottish National Gallery

In Playfair's gallery, a broad canvas sucks the eye
into its portal (curtained in deepest hues of contusion),
where three archpresbyters of flesh take centre stage.

Even those who glance away already feel the scene
branded on their psyche, sense it haunting dreams,
spinning lonely paranoias.

Dare to watch! These allopathic men
squint back, observe our recoil from their ghoulish aura,
forms lit as if by marsh gas.

Ashen-faced, in blue and green scrubs, fresh
blood on their gloves, they'll admit
whomsoever will enter this theatre,

surrendered to the mind's reductive glimmer.
(Here's no mystery of the soul – scripts hold disease
to be the clockwork's malfunction.)

Sleight of hand, and an anaesthetist brings the body
down … like Theseus minus Ariadne's counsel …
into the labyrinth, where it lies

supine on the sterile altar, and surgeons flourish silver
instruments, make their paramedian incisions
through skin and subcutaneous fat.

Within lies the metastatic lump, which they debulk,
scraping malignant tissue with a small curette.
Little is known of Patient X –

what makes her tick.
Steady as we go! The surgeons work to fix her up, plying
their neat sutures. All being well, X will be cured,

live a long life on remission,
never to return
to that inhospitable terrain.

2. Pink Ribbons

After the film by Léa Pool

Waiting in the wings,
an industry rallying women
to combat breast cancer
with pink – buying it
in specially branded things:
{trinkets, ear muffs,
furry dice, a range of car
accessories, key rings} –
armies of pink women:
victims, survivors,
friends, and supporters,
all doing their bit,
jogging round Westminster
by night (while more MPs
than usual are sleeping),
raising a small fortune
for big pharma's 'Cure'
that's always on the brink
of being found
and meanwhile enjoys

presumed success
by dyeing the world pink.

3. Outing the Mafia

Behind the scenes 'The Big C''s executive producers –
the boys alluded to, but rarely ever named.

First-off, Nuclear Radiation is sinister and invisible,
likes to infiltrate his prey, brooding,

often waiting years to strike. His brother,
Air Pollution, specialised in spewing

particulates and dioxins, is similarly imperceptible
except on hot days in cities,

when with shimmering hands he chokes his victims.
The cousin, Agro Chemical, sporting skull

and crossbones, is quite different – a garrulous type
who sprays pesticides as he peddles GMOs, insisting

the world would starve if it weren't for him.
Then there's slick godfather Mr Postmodern Living,

on his arm an ironic supermarket basket
of products that stir up Bloody Toxic (body

as cocktail shaker); ingredients: nail polish, air fresheners,
tinned food, sunscreen, fizzy drinks, dry-cleaned suits,

processed meat, underarm deodorants – this inside job
quietly conspiring to damage DNA, disrupt hormones, inflame

tissues, switch genes on or off. Meanwhile, the trouble
and strife, Mrs Suppressed Emotion, keeps calm,

carries on running to meet hubby's every need. Such good
fellas, with multiple politicians, lobbyists, and admen

in their pockets, these Mafiosi are brilliantly adept
at spreading tumours, at not playing fair.

MOTHER HAIKU,
FROM *WINTER JOURNAL, 2013–2014*

This incessant rain –
the world feels each wound & bleeds
hurt that I observe.

*

Toes burn with chilblains –
raw genetic legacy
from my mother's side.

*

News comes – her cancer
has crept into the bones, sits
gnawing the marrow.

*

Bare twigs, strange mildness
makes me wish for blizzards, white-
out – the bite of frost.

*

I cut my hair short,
disguise badly shorn layers
under scarves & hats.

*

My Rose bears fresh shoots –
so early? I prune them off,
fear it won't grow back.

*

Distance ... *Mother, you*
must be home – I call again,
leave a brief message.

*

Rusty, b r o k e n sieve –
ripped heart-mesh through which there drips
a sap of sorrow.

*

Streets are now awash –
turned a mad spring of longing
for some connection.

PAIN THRESHOLD

Here at this cracked door – its paint-flakes, its broken mortise –
she holds her bowl like Gormley's statue in the flooded crypt.
Look, a few drops prised out! Still she waits. Is it fortitude she
lacks? At this threshold she's stood many times before.

At last a voice calls: 'Who dares?' And she wonders, *who would
willingly enter*? Many place distraction before the work required.
But there's a growing horde prepared to press the ancient timber
… *ah, solidarity with these bleeding hearts!* The door's rusted hinges
judder.

Darklands, where demons snipe with vicious claws, and scars
break open to be licked with acrid tongues. Around her, like a
phantom scaffold, derelict frameworks, which she clung to, can at
last be dismantled. Only these hands! But every nail, every cut
acknowledges the pain. As she labours, others pass in trails of
tears. Bathing in warm waters, their limbs float like weeds.
Together they'll prepare poultices of comfrey and myrrh.

PRAYER FOR GRIEF

Unstoppable now these truant drops rising beneath the eyelids, coursing into creases of the face, hot streams, and the relief, blended with embarrassment – the body spontaneously springing a leak, like pissing oneself as an adult, and in full sobriety.

Be gone purse-lip of fear! Stay sensations in the belly, the diffuse ache, a longing like a parched Toad in a concrete garden. May grief be a familiar, righteous response to pain, to the insane way we live – every tear brushed into a jade bowl for blessing, then restored to the ocean, where our souls are strong enough to swim.

III. THE SKIN OF THEIR FUTURE

'We do not inherit the Earth from our ancestors, we borrow it from our children.'

Source uncertain

CLIMATE SCIENTIST SPEAKS

> 'The Sibyl, with frenzied mouth uttering things not
> to be laughed at, unadorned and unperfumed, yet
> reaches to a thousand years with her voice by aid of
> the god.'
>
> Heraclitus

Our integrated Earth system is a thing of beauty –
the work of algorithms and differential equations.
In the calm of the lab, I sit by a plasma screen observing
the kaleidoscopic patterns of sea ice concentrations.
Through the laws and logic focusing my mind,
I peer into the future.

Arachne, our super-computer, makes 600 trillion calculations
per second, weaves scenes of spiralling instability.
With a tap on my touchscreen, I look through distant eyes in the sky:
polar orbiters that monitor deep-water currents, surface
temperatures, and melting rates of glaciers and ice sheets.
Data drops into my office like subterranean water
in a limestone cave, leaving ever more profound impressions.

Often I'm gazing thousands of years into the past,
analysing cryospheric systems, evidence from borings in ice caps,
those giant glassy scrolls chronicling periods of global heating
and cooling. Unforeseen results appear like rays of sunlight
piercing the atrium of a temple; then my mind fledges hypotheses
that rise on thermal currents. I race to track them down,
start the next phase of rigorous assessment.

When the media publish my findings, or I report with colleagues
to Congress, there's always the hope that this time
our work will make a difference. Mostly I feel as if I'm speaking
with addicts on the subject of their habit –

44

the harm it's doing them and others, the denial of this truth.
Back home, I well up as my kids play at being adults –
their make-believe shaped by the only world they know.

O, but my angels, the unravelling web ...

MIDSUMMER HEAT

Beak ajar, a Blackbird on a fence
holds out its wings, as if shirking off
a heavy coat – this, a form of panting.
Soon it rises into the cool reaches
of a large Horse Chestnut.

*

In a park, a tinder of kids
smoulders in the pocket shade
of a sapling.
Keeping bigger trees might breach
the children's health & safety.

MIGRANT NEIGHBOURS

They occupy airspace round our tall Victorian houses,
wheeling, calling in a shrill, mysterious tongue, a ruckus born up
by hot winds from Africa, stirring with quixotic behaviour.

Out walking I met a brown-skinned man in a striped polo shirt
pointing at a tree. 'Look, Wood Pigeon nest inside!'
Peering through a screen of foliage, I glimpsed it

and thanked him for sharing the secret. 'Bird don't trust
foreigner!' he replied, waving his camera.
O, white, small-town England …

Sickle-shaped, mercurial, my migrant neighbours
were once called 'Devil Birds'. Like scimitars
slicing through fixed trajectories –

human lives invested in bricks, mortgages ('pledges of death'),
soulless work for cruise-line retirement – Swifts are harbingers
of repressed dimensions.

Icarus, have we not learnt? Literalising the spirit's flight,
every summer, crowds amass in thrall to the Red Arrows –
white male egos spewing patriotic vapour

to suck more youth into the wide-mouthed war machine.
Whistling in our dreams, Swifts soar to 10,000 feet and sleep
on the wing. Daily they return to press us –

theirs no choreographed routine, but ceaseless
improvisations with each other, with wind currents, insects;
I listen, try to interpret.

TIP #5: WHAT NOT TO SAY WHILE ONLINE DATING

'It is the responsibility of the poet to be a woman   to keep an eye on
                    this world and cry out like Cassandra, but be
                    listened to this time.'

Grace Paley, 'Responsibility'

Was he 'Jetstream Dreamer –

> *high-flying, airy, turbulent,*
> *quirky, dramatic, tempestuous?'*

(Not with that headline deluging adjectives.)

> Perhaps he was Bluefooted Booby, Surfguy, Machinewash40,
> Shipshape, Weatherman, Neptune? She can't recall –

but she was a green-hearted woman, seeking a soulmate,

> & it was a first exchange, him recounting the previous night –
> Beaufort 9 bludgeoning Bristol, pounding the city

like WWII was recurring. On the Harbourside,

> gales chucking slops at houseboats, yachts,
> clinking masts like Chinese businessmen gan-bei-ing a deal,

while up at a window, him inhaling the freshness –

> he loved a good storm for clearing the air.
> *Yes,* she messaged, *but here on the Somerset border*

I saw a giant python swallowing the street – just inches from my feet

its grey, liquid body tumbling rubbish & a stink of sewage.
Then, warming to the theme, she voiced her fear

of British rains changing, importing larger inundations.

With hindsight, she can see why he didn't reply;
for a man after romance, her words may have alarmed –

signalled a *frigid, hysterical, man-eating Cassandra.*

MIMESIS/NEMESIS

For Ophrys apifera

In the meadow that slopes
to an aching stream,

we're pilgrims come to reverence
        this mythical plant – a chimera
that's animal & vegetable in form.

        But the tractor's already made its bid
for silage,
        & from the margins, rattles round robotic –

        Krone arm bearing down
where grasses quake & fall,

                this Keridwen come before her time
        gnashing teeth,

her galvanised desires
        mutated beyond the ancient rites
of husbandry.

        We rush in where angels knelt;
    this dwindling haven
                from which still ascend

                        on slender spears
                sepals colour of white-girl
                        nipples, where each

corolla's russet fuzz
is scented
eau de female Bee;

has stubby flightless
wings our quivering
fingers touch.

How could such beings evolve so
wily in mimesis,
yet seem so innocent
of their nemesis closing now?

These ever-decreasing circles –
Krone a swarm
maddened by the smog
of ancient sunlight –

in the meadow that slopes
to an aching stream.

HOW WE SLEEP AT NIGHT

'the two primary sins of Western civilisation:
amnesia and anaesthesia'

Francis Weller

It's not just the swift-action pills
knocked back with a double shot of whisky
that block the demons, the shakes –
all that squats below the surface;

or booze, dope, & other drugs
that numb us through, switch off the mind,
where pharmed-up Monkeys' eyes
are burned, appear on random loop.

Nor's it just the neuroleptic telly,
tabloids dragging tattooed Winehouse bones
round the walls of Camden;
or the new fundamentalisms
that deny the senses, the bacchanals,
ecstatic flight –

but at root, it's the prickly, nauseous fear
of peering in the pit. There, like harrowed Sows
in metal crates, our souls are pressed
while Piglets wade through blood & shit
with amputated t e e t h.

ANTLER

Leaf litter parting like a Dog's damp yawn
around teeth of bleached coral, or

a lump of ossified Lichen, which curious hands
lift to reveal the nub end

of an antler – cragged as blistered paint, wax
dribbled on a withered branch,

one side of its fork splintered to a sharp
point, as if broken in a fight.

Seizing their prize, the children clamp it
to their heads, become

demented unicorns with bifurcated horns,
and, scrambling for more

treasure in the underfoot graveyard, their bare
fingers search the wet, black layers,

young detectives combing for bones. Finding ribs,
skull, vertebrae, they're soon piecing

Deer together, as if willing life into a corpse –
solemn undertakers working

backwards in time. Task complete, they ask
if I'll photograph this wonder –

its two legged, upside-down pelvis, ribs like barbs
jutting from its backbone, skull crowned

with one broken antler. Then, as if measuring
themselves against their own

inner creature, they lie beside it –
unconsciously rehearsing death, the battles

they may fight,
leaps they'll make into the skin of their future.

DOLL HEADS

After Marian Bruce

Voodoo feeling –

these bronzed heads   on springs
a bunch of jacks & jills   burst from their boxes
broken babies, open-mouthed – unweaned
mutely screaming   wanting me
to help them. Disturbing on their tray, the many-
headed hydra of society today – cut, served upon
this platter, this severance of distress, a thousand thousand left
to fend for themselves   their absent mothers
caught in trauma   some generations back
bleeding from their breasts   bereft creatures
these the orphans   infants shut
crying in their cots, till grief & anger
walls up inside
walls them up inside

O, how they hang in the balance   on these
mortal coils – silent agonies trapped in their missing
throats. They're alone   & only   we
can see them, feel their harsh reproaches
resonate within. All these children clamouring
to be   shock-headed peters   & paulines
with hollow eyes   open mouths, these hungry
ghosts   their absent bellies
the aching of the world   to be allowed

How can I help these children seeking birth
into a world shrinking from their grasp? What crumbs
will we leave them? Sometimes I cannot see
a dab of bread & milk   being left

O, this agony of wanting   of trying to make myself
a safe container. (Come, come little ones
into my heart's dark house! In each ventricle, each
chamber you can rest.)

Ah, ah, here their cries will   cease,
their hungers find appeasement
as each head shrinks to be the grit   endured within flesh

IV. LEGACIES

'We must enter the healing ground as elders who have been seasoned by grief, recognising we carry soul medicine for those who are beginning their apprenticeship. Perhaps now we can begin to build a new culture, one that honours soul and the soul of the world.'

Francis Weller, *The Wild Edge of Sorrow*

THE SCOLD'S BRIDLE

i.m. E.J.M, 1940–2014

Gerard, the hospice chaplain, said our parents
       can be our greatest teachers – all of us enrolled
in life for the soul's 'higher' education.

       Mother, now your spirit is loosed,
has travelled invisible realms – is welcomed to become
       'one with all that's love, truth, light,

where hurt and wounds are cleansed in love's fire' –
       I'm learning from the blood-tie we shared.
As death approached, you were stoic, and I massaged your hands

       when words could not be found. So much never said – secrets
and silence the way most women of your time, your class
       survived. Yet ghosts of voices linger …

*

Don't rock the boat!

Put up & shut up!

Try to be more lady-like!

Lie   back & think of England!

*

The day after you passed,
            a girlfriend and I up the wild, ancient hill –
                in March wind and rain, us rattling, drumming,
                bee-humming on deerskin, fire leaping at our feet,

as I hailed my ancestors –
            all those in my lineage
                who never nurtured their spark – creativity
                thwarted by duty
                            and the mute effect
                                of buried trauma.

            From the hillside I called you,
                                    Spirit-allies,
as four Buzzards wheeled above our heads, a flock of avian angels
            for this 'black sheep' in white skin –

        I, that rebel-child …
                and still as adult,
                                the ache to exorcise
                    parental snipes & social judgement.

                        *

                Who do you think you are?

                        Wasting your education …

                (Clenched iron of lower jaw,
                gums raw, bleeding …)

                You're being a SELFISH BITCH!

        (Head with its ache of armoured cage,
                all that unexpressed
RAGE …)

And: *Don't wash your dirty linen in public!*

(Read: *Lock away all skeletons & discard the key!*)

Or: *Avoid being so political/spiritual/female!*

i.e.:   *DON'T DARE CHALLENGE US!*

*

Yet, Mother, you imparted wealth –
        from my cot, the rhyming nonsense
wooed from my lips; Carroll, Lear, and bedtime stories;

your *toothless wifie,* and other voices
        disguising yours defined
by that *'baby blues'* diagnosis ...

*

(*For valour, Mrs Moore,
                just keep taking the Valium ...*)

*

You as mimic, actress manquée
        holding court at the dinner table –
the family ear for French, and thirst for the praise of strangers.

        Schooled to select an identity
of nurse or secretary,
        your shorthand & typing speeds beat the average;

but for your firstborn, life brought choices
        you'd never imagined – and, Mother,
how did that sit?

Despite feelings you'd never admit, the prizes you bestowed
for school success – a dictionary, a thesaurus, & a volume
of MacNeice, when I loved 'Prayer before Birth' –

encouraged me, and I honour this in writing
my 'prayer after death' as your body returns
(star-dust garnered from galaxies),

as cells no longer hold the fire
that bore me into the world. Between my fingers,
those bird-bones of hands

which fed me, brushed my downy hair, washed my small
frame. For this, Mother-Ancestor,
words unbound like rivers to the ocean ...

*

Harpy. Shrew. Witch ...
all the untold
stories,
all the souls denied
by the 'scold's bridle'

NARAWARN & THE SEA

> 'Our hearts feel bugrabanya (broken to pieces) as we
> remember the stories of the marri bayi (big kill),
> galgala (small pox) and mubi (mourning). But we
> who ngalawa (remain) must honour our peoples &
> countries through baya yurring (speaking true).'
> Uncle Charles Madden, Cadigal Elder, Sydney, 2014

Long time ago when this world was new, the land was dry &
barren. No water, no plants, no animals, no life. Up in the sky,
Arilla & Narawarn, two brothers didn't get along. That old tale of
sibling rivalry, Narawarn often goading his older brother. One
day Arilla punched him hard on the nose – a blow that knocked
Narawarn clean from the sky. From the arid wastes below, he
called mournfully for help. Heart filled with pity & regret, Arilla
leant down to scoop him up. But he was too far away & Arilla
couldn't risk tumbling down himself. Alone in the bone dryness
of rock, Narawarn began to cry. Fat drops that plopped from his
nose & soon became a pool moistening his toes. Still his sorrow
flowed – billions of tears rushing out through the dusty expanses,
a salty river widening, deepening, stretching to the horizon. Soon
it began rocking back & forth, a maternal motion that brought him
some comfort. Seeing this first sea, Arilla turned himself into the
wind. Whisking over the surface, his breath swelled the waves'
shoulders & foamed up their heads; yet his brother remained out
of reach. Lonely Narawarn begged for company, & so appeared
the marine creatures – Crabs scuttling sideways to make him
laugh; spiky Sea Urchins; brilliant Corals, Octopus, Squid, Fish in
all sizes & colours; Dolphins; Seals. In vain Arilla tried everything
to rescue him; & in his frustration he'd cause giant waves to strike
the coast. But nothing could bring Narawarn back. And that's
why our tears remain salty to this day.

LEGACY, MOTHER'S DAY, 2016

'sa glorieuse Mere / Par qui grace rien ne perit'
François Villon

Desiring life, a new world, yet seeking protection
from an injurious brother thirsting

after every drop of our parents' estate,
and in commemoration of this day,

I seek recourse beyond the law (in Blighty a parent
still has the right to disinherit a child);

and, upholding the Gallic spirit in my blood, find
justice in the poetic tradition …

*

Item, to my sibling I bequeath forgiveness, though a shabby bird
in snot-green, moth-attacked plumage. A Ringneck

Indian Parrot that escaped an owner's cage, it's survived
two Sydney winters, visits the garden squawking for food.

I cut and core an apple, remove the pips, place the offering.
At its slow sidle down a branch, I click my tongue,

coax it on. Foreign here, no prospect of a mate, it possesses little
instinct to survive, is convict runaway requiring compassion.

*

Item, to my sibling too – the scrutiny of Australia's Sun. Minus
shades, the shadows that we drag become more visible.

Against this bright world of white-gold beaches, turquoise bays,
ripe fruit, vivid clothes, open-air markets,

the contrast of a dark, sack-like shape – that stash
of unexamined life. In the heat this rotting burden

taints the body and the soul, while mentally it fuels an arsenal –
projectiles for a triggered finger. Brother, let in the light!

ADDERWELL

An old man, who remembers old ways,
shut away, where he can't belong.

I come to him, kneel by his greasy chair,
tentative, slugged by stagnant air –

dayroom mute before jaunty TV wiles;
sunlight falling through disused minds;

shafts of stale urine. At first, flicks of lust,
pink-rimmed eyes alighting on my flesh.

But there's knowledge I desire, so I make him
Fisher King – see a moth-like hand

flicker to a fire kindling through his face.
Then he opens dried-up lips to show

what's still closed inside. Boy scrumping Russets.
Boy cycling out of town for beds of peppery

Watercress – bundles teased into his satchel.
Boy with Rabbit for an empty pot. Wild boy

who knew damp burrows near the Frome
where once Adders lurked. Did he, dared on

by others, dip his head into darkness?
(Some unconscious rite of passage?)

> *Snake, show me how to enter places*
> *where light can barely pierce …*

Old man, take me back before the neat, brick
estate – take me back to Adderwell.

FROME-SELWOOD, AN ODYSSEY

1. Forest-travelling through time

Below thick crusts of road,
> the stone cobbles of Catherine Hill,
> > foundations of Frome,
hints of a presence
> in which we find & know ourselves.

> In the heart of the town,
> > Saxonvale –
> (the road-sign implies early pastoral,
September's swineherds shaking boughs of Oak,
> raining acorns into their Pigs' avid mouths);

> this derelict place now,
> > where stoned NEETS daub grafitti,
and campaigns ignite against

> > > corvid
> > > supermarket bosses
> > > picking

> > > over rust and stone carcasses
> > of former industry,

> a wet dream of town-centre stores

> > > > gleaming
> > clean as bones.

> Yet, for self-determination,
> > call to mind roots –
> this once wooded valley

of *Sealhwudu,*
dense sallow wood
that kept waves of invaders
at bay;

Sealhwudu ...

(say it as charm, invocation, call to power!)

*

Selwood School,
Selwood Road,
& former printworks –

names like rhizomes in the local hive mind,
fragments of rotten wood
riddled with cargoes of knowledge,
all that came before.

Beneath the library – where people pore over pages,
fingering fibres of wood pulp –

ancient forest flora: Wood Anemone,
Bluebell, Yellow Archangel – soil a dispassionate
archive of seeds. Squatting patiently, they ache
to be opened,
read by sun
& rain;

while trees bursting up through cracks
yearn to interweave a canopy
beyond the highest roofs.

*

Sealhwudu ...

Southwesterlies blow in,
      summer showers needling the ground
      as water draining down
                returns to source,
         recalls the thirsty suck
               of Willow, Lime, Oak,

              fresh springs that coursed
         down steeply wooded hills ...

(dense clumps of houses, shops).

      On Cheap Street it spills into the silvery leat
         which shines like the axe
        brought to serve the Saxon cross:

           Aldhelm, the Conqueror,

        his vision of a church
            built within the forest,

               which soon spawned
                  the town.

              O Sealhwudu ...

         *

St Aldhelm's Well, King Street, dressed each May
      by children at the bidding
         of St John's officials –

their paintings and flowers an
      echo/erasure
         of an older culture's rituals;

here, the flowing mossy jaws of a lion,
over which a sign:
'Water is ██fit for a████king.

Sealhwudu …

On the bridge into town,
the River House straddling the flow
serves latte and as lookout
for Kingfishers, Otters
by a knot of River Friends.

Sealhwudu …

Across the street stands the Blue Boar Inn –
the former drinking hole
of bristly tribes
that squelched
on the riverbank
and loudly drank their fill.

Sealhwudu …

Down the Market Place,
the chain chemist sits
(stockpiling packets of industrial pills)
where clumps of Meadowsweet
were once prolific, with Woundwort, Nettle
and Willow bark aspirin,
a living pharmacopeia –

opus of millennia.

O Sealhwudu …

*

Eve's herbs,
the people's medicine
and our history of cunning men and women
demonised
as witches –

(*1731, East Woodlands,*
a woman accused of causing fits in a child
is tied to a rope and ducked in the millpond

… dies of shock and cold.)

2016, Frome – on North Parade, the Natural Health Clinic
may now promote,   under the strictest EU regulation,

complementary medicine.

O Sealhwudu …

*

To be hunters and gatherers is imprinted in our DNA:

roving in search of nuts, fruits, berries, vines, mushrooms,
our forebears knew a complex, living store
of food and remedies for ailments,
our bloodlines thus adapting for thousands of years.

Now the supermarket stands in place of the forest;
blindly we forage among shelves,
assailed by a false complexity of
colours & chemicals

for which we pay.

O Sealhwudu …

2. Forests of the Psyche

The forest still dwells in our imaginations –
 briar thickets entangling our clothes, hair –
exists as darkest nightmare, with Wolves
 and Wild Cats, Bears waking from hibernation;
this place where we're still Hansel and Gretel
 traumatised and seeking dissolved trails of crumbs.

Deeper still it inhabits the psyche,
 is the wild being we barely know
we are. Wolf in the belly snarling awake
 when the mind is tricked. On the dance floor,
gyrating, shaking, stomping, I'm
 She-Bear romping in primeval woodland glades.

3. The Elephant Beech

St John's cemetery, 24 June 2016

Strange to fell an ancient tree at Midsummer
 (limbs toppling as Frome awoke to news of Brexit).

 '… overhanging footpaths …'

Latest tomographic surveys assured councillors of hollowing
 heartwood that could not support the overall structure.

 '… families walking to and from school …'

Passers-by see deus ex machina, helmeted arborists lifted
 on a metal arm, frenzied saws cutting boughs like cheese.

 'They've butchered it …'

Riddled with fungus, the tree was habitat for birds, bats, insects,
  its purply-green crown majestic alongside the church.

> *'Now each time I pass I want to weep...'*

In some cultures, veterans, supported with braces, poles, struts,
  are venerated for the wisdom they inspire.

> *'I don't know how to put my hurt into words ...'*

People held a wake, with roses placed round bunions, dimples,
  candles cradled in the roots.

> *'The District Council can't afford the cost of litigation.'*

A 12 ft stump, this last tree dreaming. Behind it, St John's spire
  is a raised dagger, a golden cockerel crying on its point:

> *'Nature is the living, visible garment of God.'*

4. Tree-planting song

Whatcombe Community Fields, Frome

Next weekend we'll go there
with boots, spades, and trowels,
help the kids to dig the saplings
in through the matted turf.

The wind may blow, birds may sing,
and hands will get muddy; afterwards,
with glowing cheeks and snug
on bales, we'll eat bread and soup.

And who will be the last to leave?
(Who will be the last to leave?)

And will you be the last to leave
a legacy for healing the future?

5. Scars

Vallis Veg, Frome

Stripped to iron bones, red-grey, torched of paint, flayed
by flames, a thing of strange beauty, yet the toxic uproar
that seared the night gave fright to roosting birds, singed
a grove of young Oaks, charred their trunks – this final
call on a wild jaunt, the out-of-town trip, pale green faces
propelled through windows, air funnelling foreheads, jaws,
the steep lane diving to the woods, Deer's leap
across their path, high minds reliving game action fantasy.
Then *Shit, man, where next? Left? Right?* Backseat
boy-rider seizes control, screeching wheels, cattle grid bone-
shaker, the track uphill, car grinds into first, tyres slowing
up the grassy path, and suddenly, nowhere else to go – gate
barred – jolting halt amidst the budding wood, bailing out
lairy like jostling Cockerels. Then *What if?* setting in
at the cops finding prints. Casual match is flicked in the tank.
BOOM! Whoops and jelly legs dissolve into darkness.

*

A tractor towed the carcass away, took it for scrap;
and now younger kids, wide-eyed on the way to Forest School,
stare at the trees, shoes scuffing burnt ground, shattered
glass. We write messages, hang pictures, treat the Oaks
like injured patients, hope they'll get well soon.

And these adolescent natives, planted on pasture, will one day speak
of this kindness – not in words, but stirred by southerly breezes,
when children grown to adulthood, grandchildren horseyed-up
on shoulders, seek the deep shade. There, fingers tracing scars,
a body-prayer of arms embraces one large girth.

DEVIL'S ROPE

'Barbed wire used properly can be a beautiful sight.'
Donald Trump

Vicious gibbet, Crow hanging by a tendon in her foot,
snagged, we surmised, as she landed on the wire –
then numerous attempts to free herself, wings beseeching the air,
excavations of pain deep within her brain.

Collateral crucifixion; we could barely speculate
on the time it took to die. Now, beak pointing at the ground,
leg muscles torn, claws set round the barb
in an improvised 'e' ('e' for epitaph, 'e' for entreaty),

the wind mocks Crow's former vitality, ruffling
greyish down, lifting the stiff, pleated feathers,
twitching her tail. Later I return to vigil with her, seated
on the grassy bank beside the horses' pasture –

this silent wake on lunar Beltane, the Sun
etching steel clouds over Midlothian – and touch
a veil of horror hanging round the black cadaver,
mourn this mirror of our culture's darkness.

Earlier you'd affirmed my capacity to face the world's suffering
and yet to love. Moved by this observation and sorrow,
tears flow in streaks as I lift my face to the sky – a peripheral
awareness of Mare and Stallion ambling across.

Tender scoops of nostril huff in the scent of death,
then, rising over the devil's rope, a pair of equine angels
snuffle with velvet lips at my cheeks, stand in slow communion –
'e' for empathy, 'e' for ennoblement of Crow.

'TEARS I SHED YESTERDAY HAVE BECOME RAIN'

'Moisture pouring in and through and out of you, of
me, in the vast poem of the hydrological cycle.'
John Seed & Joanna Macy, 'Gaia Meditation'

Trees for Life, Dundreggan

in low boats of cloud harboured in the tree-ringed mountains,
in the Bracken, Ling, Bell Heather that cling to bare peaks,
in ancient Oak, Scots Pine, Aspen, Alder, Birch,
in purple Blaeberry juice staining our hands,
in a burn's icy milk charging a gorge,
in gilded clarity of pools –
tears I shed

in boggy trickles,
red hairy Sundew, Butterwort leaves
spread like skins of small, green bananas,
in Meadowsweet, in Orchid, in dusky yellow stars
of St John's Wort, in a Birch stump with Polypore hard
as granite hooves, in the Dragonfly perched by the loch,
in people replanting the Caledonian Forest – tears I've shed

in Red Squirrel, Pine Marten, Crested Tit, in guts of a Toad
crushed on the road, in tourists pedalling through the glen,
in the Water Avens' claret petals, in the Moriston's
broad expanse, in snouts of Wild Boar
rootling on its banks, in Hare-
bell, in Eyebright –
tears I shed

in Foxgloves
nodding by the wall, in fairy
horns of Lichen, pale as snuff, in the dawn

mists encircling the yurt on this day
of my departure – tears
of the Great Heart
pulsing in all.

NOTES

Biophony, Prior to Invasion
'Waran' is the Dharug name for Sydney Cove. Dharug is an Australian Aboriginal language from the Sydney area. See Dharug and Dharawal Dalang website.

A British Marine Officer Considers the Colonial Presence,
Ventriloquising the 'Natives'
This poem is based on the accounts of British officers of the First Fleet, namely Watkin Tench and William Dawes, who recorded their impressions of the first phase of colonisation and tried to learn the 'Indians'' language.

'A Tear Is an Intellectual Thing'
The title is a line from Blake's poem 'The Grey Monk'. 'When I from black and he from white cloud free...' is from 'The Little Black Boy'. When Britain's First Fleet of thirteen hundred convicts, guards, and administrators invaded Australia in January 1788, the Eora people (comprising the area's three main clans, the Cadigal, Wanegal, and Cammeraygal) numbered about fifteen hundred. Expropriation, destruction of their natural food sources, smallpox, and murder caused around seventy per cent of the local Sydney population to perish during the eighteenth century alone.

Daughter of the Dissolution
'Wiyanga' and 'biyanga' are the Dharug words for 'mother' and 'father'. Moorooboora was father to 'Cora Gooseberry' and leader of the Murro-ore-dial clan; the place name Maroubra, a beachside suburb in Sydney, is an echo of his presence.

Trafficked Women Drown off French Coast
The British government's long-term programme of ethnic cleansing in Scotland is evidenced in numerous ways, including the

Statutes of Iona, passed in 1609, with provisions such as the out-lawing of bards and other bearers of traditional culture and the enforced education of clan chiefs' heirs in Lowland schools, where they had to learn to speak, read, and write English. The 1746 Act of Proscription's 'Dress Act' also prohibited traditional wearing of clan tartan and kilts. In 1852, Sir Charles Trevelyan, Secretary to HM Treasury and co-founder of the Highland & Island Emigra-tion Society, wrote in a letter to the society's other founder, Sir John McNeill, that '"A national effort" would now be necessary in order to rid the land of the surviving Irish and Scotch Celts.'

Black House, Great Berneray, Western Isles
A blackhouse is a traditional type of thatched house once common in the Scottish Highlands and Hebrides. The origin of the name is unclear. It may have been a racial slur used by the Lowland Scots and English to promote the notion of the Gaels' supposed inferior-ity. It could also have been a confusion between the Gaelic words 'dubh', meaning 'black', and 'tughadh', meaning 'thatch', since Gaelic was regularly mistranslated and anglicised. "s na h-igheanan nam 'badan sàmhach/a' dol a Clachan mar o thus' are lines from Sorley MacLean's poem 'Hallaig'. He translates them from the Gaelic as 'and the girls in silent bands/go to Clachan as in the beginning'. A clachan is a traditional village settlement.

In 1847 Queen Victoria and Prince Albert cruised around the Western Isles on board HMY *Victoria & Albert*. Victoria's diary of her experiences, *Leaves from the Journal of Our Life in the Highlands*, makes a passing remark about the famines affecting people there at the time. On 19 August she writes, 'The inhabitants of these islands have, unhappily, been terrible sufferers during the last winter from famine.' But she does not consider the causes, nor does she make any connection with Lord Salisbury's purchase of some of the islands, despite having mentioned it. Rather her focus is the Hebrides' romantic appeal: 'the Western lochs and isles ... are so beautiful, and so full of poetry and romance, traditions and historical associations'.

Five years later, she donated £300 from the Privy Purse to as-sist the dispossessed in emigrating to Australia through the High-

79

land & Island Emigration Society (of which Albert was patron) – through loans that emigrants were expected to pay back. Correspondence between members of this society indicates that there was a pressing need for labour in the new colony, particularly to shepherd its vast flocks (in 1852 seven million Sheep in New South Wales alone) and to return their fleeces for the Mother Country's burgeoning textile industries.

Teenage Skate Punk

A bora ground is a sacred site for Aboriginal initiation rites. One of the first to be identified by the British was at Woccanmagully, which in 1788 they seized to establish their first farm. Now generally known as 'Farm Cove', the site lies in Sydney's Botanic Gardens, adjacent to the Opera House. During my visits, I found no sign indicating the site's Aboriginal significance. 'Karadjis' refers to Aboriginal shamans and tradition bearers.

'A State of Possession Already Existing Beyond the Memory of [Hu]Man[s]'

The poem title is adapted from a chapter heading in Andy Wightman's book *The Poor Had No Lawyers*. A commonty is, in Scots Law, a common; a piece of land in which two or more persons have a common right. In Scotland currently, just 2.5 per cent of the land is community owned; large-scale private land ownership is concentrated in the hands of a few individuals, including the Queen.

Mimesis/Nemesis

Krone is a make of agricultural machinery.

Narawarn & the Sea

After the Aboriginal creation story 'Narawarn & the Coming of the Sea' from the Dharawal Grandmothers. I heard it told by Auntie Julie Freeman in a film at the First Australians Galleries, Australian Museum, Sydney.

A Legacy, Mother's Day, 2016
'sa glorieuse Mere / Par qui grace rien ne perit' are lines from *Le Lais* (*The Legacy*) by the fifteenth-century French poet François Villon. They are translated by Peter Dale (in the Penguin Classics edition of Villon's *Selected Poems*) as 'Our Lady's Grace/that leaves no soul for lost'.

Frome-Selwood, an Odyssey
Frome-Selwood is an old name for the English market town of Frome. NEETs is an acronym referring to young people under twenty-five and not in education, employment, or training. 'Sealhwudu' is the Saxon word for 'sallow wood', which described the ancient forest of Selwood, surviving in fragments and place names around Frome. 'Nature is the living, visible garment of God' is a quote from Goethe.

'Tears I Shed Yesterday Have Become Rain'
The title is a line from the Vietnamese Zen Buddhist monk and poet Thich Nhat Hanh, in 'Message' (from *Call Me by My True Names*, his collected poems).

ACKNOWLEDGEMENTS

Versions of poems in this collection first appeared in the following publications, whose editors I thank: 'Antler', 'Doll Heads', and 'Prayer for Grief' in *Unpsychology Magazine*; 'Migrant Neighbours' and 'The Big C' in *Shearsman Magazine*; 'Devil's Rope' in *Black Box Manifold*; 'Climate Scientist Speaks' in *Uncivilised Poetics* (Dark Mountain Project, 2016); 'First Contact' and 'Mother Tongue' in *Scintilla*; 'Tears I Shed Yesterday Have Become Rain', in *Plum Tree Tavern*; 'Biophony Prior to Invasion' in *Nature & Language* (Corbel Stone Press, 2017); 'Narawarn & the Sea' in *Nature & Myth* (Corbel Stone Press, 2017); 'Black House, Great Berneray' in *Northwords Now*; 'Mimesis/Nemesis' in *Plumwood Mountain Journal*; 'How We Sleep at Night', 'Midsummer Heat', and 'Pain Threshold' in *IN-TATTO. INTACT: Ecopoesia. Ecopoetry* (La Vita Felice, 2017); 'Tip #5: What Not to Say While Online Dating' in *Magma*.

'A Legacy, Mother's Day 2016' was awarded A\$1,000 for best poem in *Meniscus,* July 2017. 'Frome-Selwood, an Odyssey' was written as part of my residency with the Heritage Lottery funded community project Last Tree Dreaming, designed to raise awareness of the heritage of Somerset's Selwood Forest. It was first published in *Long Poem Magazine.* The first section of *The Mother Country,* 'The Disinherited', originally appeared as a limited-edition pamphlet of twelve poems *(The Disinherited,* Green Seer Books, 2018).

Massive thanks to B. Anne Adriaens, Mandy Griffiths, Lisa Fannen, and Armorel Weston for help with editing these poems. I'm grateful for the opportunity to collaborate with Awen Publications, headed up by Anthony Nanson, a talented writer, astute editor, and kindred spirit. Also for support from Alex Hart, Rebekah Arthurs, Andy Andrews, Sara Iles, Sarah Tremlett, Lindsay Clarke, D.M. Black, Rosie Jackson, Maddy Harland, Anne Elvey, Massimo D'Arcangelo, and Brian and Isobel Taylor. I acknowledge all my poetry students for the rich interactions we've shared in discussing poetry and refining craft. Lastly, deep gratitude for the encouragement of my husband, Alasdair Taylor, whose love helps make it all possible.

The quotation on p. 1 is from Frantz Fanon, *The Wretched of the Earth*, trans. Constance Farrington, Penguin, London, 2002. The quotation on p. 7. is from Lieutenant-General Watkin Tench, *1788: Watkin Tench*, ed. Tim Flannery, Text Classics, Melbourne, 2013. The quotation on p. 19 is from Sorley Maclean, 'Hallaig', in *Spring Tide and Neap Tide: Selected Poems, 1932–72*, Canongate, Edinburgh, 1977. The quotation on p. 21 is quoted with permission of the author from Michael Ventura, 'The Age of Endarkenment', author's website. The quotation from Sir John Sinclair on p. 23 is from Andy Wightman, *The Poor Had No Lawyers: Who Owns Scotland (And How They Got It)*, Birlinn, Edinburgh, 2013. The quotation on p. 35 is from Don Watson, *Caledonia Australis: Scottish Highlanders on the Frontier of Australia*, Vintage, Sydney, 1997. The quotation on p. 29 is from Denise Levertov, *The Sorrow Dance*, New Directions, New York, 1966. The quotation on p. 49 is from Grace Paley, 'Responsibility', in *A Grace Paley Reader: Stories, Essays, and Poetry*, ed. Kevin Bowen & Nora Paley, Farrar, Straus & Giroux, New York, 2017. The quotation on p. 52 is quoted with permission of the author from Francis Weller, *The Wild Edge of Sorrow: Rituals of Renewal and the Sacred Work of Grief*, North Atlantic Books, Berkeley, CA, 2015. The quotation from Uncle Charles Madden on p. 64 is from a storyboard in the First Australians Galleries, Australian Museum, Sydney. The quotation on p. 65 is from François Villon, 'Le Lais', in *Villon's Selected Poems*, trans. Peter Dale, Penguin, London, 1993. The quotation on p. 79 is from John Seed & Joanna Macy, 'Gaia Meditiation', Work that Reconnects website.

Soul of the Earth: the Awen anthology of eco-spiritual poetry
edited by Jay Ramsay

Beautifully crafted, yet challenging received wisdom and pushing boundaries, these are cutting-edge poems from a new generation of writers who share a love of the Earth and haven't given up on humans either. In poems as light as a butterfly and as wild as a storm you'll find vivid, contemporary voices that dare to explore a spiritual dimension to life on Earth and, in doing so, imply that a way out of our global crisis of ecological catastrophe, financial meltdown, and bankruptcy of the spirit is to look beyond the impasse of materialism. With contributions from poets in the USA, Canada, UK, Australia, and New Zealand, this anthology reaches out across the planet to embrace the challenges and blessings of being alive on the Earth in the twenty-first century.

'All real poetry seeks to "renew the face of the earth" – and so to resist the exploiting, banalization or defacing of what lies around us. I hope this collection will serve the renewal of vision we so badly need.'
Most Revd Dr Rowan Williams

Poetry/Spirituality ISBN 978-1-906900-17-5 £12.00

Dancing with Dark Goddesses: movements in poetry
Irina Kuzminsky

The dance is life – life is the dance – in all its manifestations, in all its sorrow and joy, cruelty and beauty. And the faces of the Dark Goddesses are many – some are dark with veiling and unknowing, some are dark with sorrow, some are dark with mystery and a light so great that it paradoxically shades them from sight. The poems in this collection are an encounter with many of these faces, in words marked with feminine energy and a belief in the transformative power of the poetic word. Spiritual and sexual, earthy and refined, a woman's voice speaks to women and to the feminine in women and men – of an openness to life, a surrender to the workings of love, and a trust in the Dark Goddesses and their ways of leading us through the dance.

'A mythological journey of archetypes.' *Richard McKane*

Poetry/Dance ISBN 978-1906900-12-0 £9.99

Pilgrimage:
a journey to Love Island
Jay Ramsay

In the summer of 1990 Jay Ramsay set out on pilgrimage with an interfaith group from London to Iona. The result is his most ambitious book-length poem, an astonishing tour de force in the tradition of Wordsworth and Chaucer. Epiphanic, conversational, meditational, psychological, political, it divines 'the cross' of spiritual and ecological being in Britain's radical tradition, as symbolised by Iona as the crown of the Celtic church and the direction that Christianity lost. Constructed as a series of 25 'days', the narrative builds symphonically like waves of the sea up to its visionary climax. Full of stories, reflections, memories, and images, Pilgrimage is above all a love poem, an invitation into the greater love that is our true becoming where we can find the God most personal to all of us – alive in the heart of Life.

Poetry/Spirituality ISBN 978-1906900-54-0 £15.00

Silver Branch:
bardic poems and letters to a young bard
Kevan Manwaring

What does it mean to write and perform bardic poetry in the twenty-first century? This monumental collection, from the author of *The Bardic Handbook* and *The Way of Awen*, brings together 25 years of selected verse to explore that challenge. The diverse range of poems can be enjoyed for their own sake and will also inspire others to craft and voice their own creative responses to identity, ecology, and community, grounded in the body, the land, and conviction. *Silver Branch* includes an introduction to the author's practice as a performance poet, originally published as *Speak Like Rain*, along with the Bardic-Chair-winning poem *Spring Fall*; *Bio*Wolf*; *Green Fire*; *Dragon Dance*; *The Taliesin Soliloquies*; *Thirteen Treasures*; poems from the stage shows *Arthur's Dream*, *Robin of the Wildwood*, *Return to Arcadia*, and *Song of the Windsmith*; plus more recent bardic poems and songs.

'Within *Silver Branch*, the ancient and modern worlds are woven together in the remaking with which we have to engage at every moment, perceiving the ancient and allowing its currency to irrigate our time and deepen our, often, surface culture.' *Caitlín Matthews*

Poetry/Mythology ISBN 978-1-906900-42-7 £16.00

Crackle of Almonds: selected poems
Gabriel Bradford Millar

In these renegade poems ranging from 1958 to 2011 Gabriel Bradford Millar presents a spectrum of life, in all its piquant poignancy, with unfaltering precision, defiance, and finesse. From the very first to the very last, the breathtaking skill of this consummate wordsmith does not waver. Many of the poems linger in the air – not least because Millar performs them orally with such verve. She believes 'that poems, like love-talk, should go from mouth to ear without any paper in between'. On the page their orality and aurality fragrance their presence without diminishing their literary elegance. Continually astonishing, these epicurean poems not only offer a lasting testimony to a 'life well-lived', but inspire the reader to live well too

'She does not just write *about* the world; she dips her syllables in the bitter sweet of its "gazpacho". She thinks melodically.' *Paul Matthews*

Poetry ISBN 978-1-906900-29-8 £9.99

Green Man Dreaming: reflections on imagination, myth, and memory
Lindsay Clarke

The transformative power of imagination, the elusive dream world of the unconscious, our changing relationship to nature, and the enduring presence of myth – these subjects have preoccupied Lindsay Clarke throughout the thirty years since he emerged as the award-winning author of *The Chymical Wedding*. Assembled in this definitive collection are the major essays, talks, and personal reflections that he has written, with characteristic verve and insight, on these and other themes relating to the evolution of consciousness in these transitional times. Speculative, exploratory, salty with wit, and interwoven with poems, this book brings the Green Man and the Daimon into conversation with alchemists, psychologists, gods, and Plains Indians, along with various poets and novelists the author has loved as good friends or as figures in the pantheon of his imagination. Through a reverie of images and ideas, *Green Man Dreaming puts* us closely in touch with the myths and mysteries that embrace our lives.

'Lindsay Clarke's magical prose elucidates the deep wisdom held at the depth of our soul … This is truly gold dust.' *Satish Kumar*

Spirituality/Mythology/Literary Criticism ISBN 978-1906900-56-4 £15.00

Ditch Vision:
essays on poetry, nature, and place
Jeremy Hooker

Ditch Vision is a book of essays on poetry, nature, and place that extends Jeremy Hooker's thinking on subjects that, as a distinguished critic and poet, he has made his life's work. The writers he considers include Edward Thomas, Robert Frost, Robinson Jeffers, Richard Jefferies, John Cowper Powys, Mary Butts, and Frances Bellerby. Through sensitive readings of these and other writers, he discusses differences between British and American writers concerned with nature and spirit of place. The book also includes essays in which he reflects upon the making of his own work as a lyric poet. Written throughout with a poet's feeling for language, *Ditch Vision* is the work of an exploratory writer who seeks to understand the writings he discusses in depth, and to illuminate them for other readers. Hooker explores the 'ground' of poetic vision with reference to its historical and mythological contexts, and in this connection *Ditch Vision* constitutes also a spiritual quest.

Literary Criticism ISBN 978-1906900-51-9 £14.00

By the Edge of the Sea:
short stories
Nicolas Kurtovitch

Nicolas Kurtovitch is one of the leading literary figures in the French-speaking country of New Caledonia in the South Pacific. The twelve short stories in By the Edge of the Sea are written with a poet's sensitivity to style and the significance of what's left unsaid. They convey an enchantment of place in their evocation of physical settings; an enchantment too of the conscious moment; a big-hearted engagement with indigenous cultures and perspectives; and arising from all these a sense of possibility permeating beyond what the eye can see. This seminal first collection of Kurtovitch's stories appears here in English for the first time, together with an introduction to the author's work and New Caledonian background.

'This collection of stories retains its appeal and importance, its freshness, a quarter-century after it first appeared, and that can now be appreciated for the first time by an English-speaking public thanks to Anthony Nanson's careful and sensitive translation.' *Peter Brown*

Fiction ISBN 978-1-906900-53-3 £9.99

Places of Truth:
journeys into sacred wilderness
Jay Ramsay

Poet and psychotherapist Jay Ramsay has been drawn to wild places all his writing life, in search of a particular deep listening experience. 'Trwyn Meditations', a sequence set in Snowdonia, begins this 24-year odyssey. 'By the Shores of Loch Awe' takes us to the fecund wilds of Scotland. 'The Oak' celebrates an ancient tree in the heart of the Cotswolds. 'The Sacred Way' is an evocation of Pilgrim Britain. 'Culbone' records the hidden history of the smallest parish church in England in a steep North Somerset valley near where Coleridge wrote 'Kubla Khan'. The final sequences, 'The Mountain' and 'Sinai', takes us beyond, in all senses, touching the places where we find I and Self.

Poetry ISBN 978-1-906900-40-3 £12.00 Spirit of Place Volume 4

The Immanent Moment
Kevan Manwaring

The sound of snow falling on a Somerset hillside, the evanescence of a waterspout on a remote Scottish island, the invisible view from a Welsh mountain, the light on the Grand Canal in Venice, the fire in a Bedouin camelherder's eyes … These poems consider the little epiphanies of life and capture such fleeting pulses of consciousness in sinuous, euphonic language. A meditation on time, mortality, transience, and place, this collection celebrates the beauty of both the natural and the man-made, the familiar and the exotic, and the interstices and intimacy of love.

Poetry ISBN 978-1-906900-41-0 £8.99

Tidal Shift: selected poems
Mary Palmer

Knowing her end was near, Mary Palmer worked on her poems, compiling her very best and writing new ones with a feverish intensity. This is the result, published here with her full cooperation and consent. These are poems from the extreme edge and very centre of life – words of light that defy death's shadow with a startling intensity, clarity, and honesty. Containing poems from across Mary's career, selected by Jay Ramsay, *Tidal Shift* is an impressive legacy from a poet of soul and insight.

Poetry ISBN 978-1-906900-09-0 £9.99